Renewal
POEMS BY IRVIN DESIR

PAPILLOTE PRESS
London and Trafalgar, Dominica

© Estate Irvin Desir 2026

The moral right of Irvin Desir to be identified as the author of this work has been asserted by him in accordance with the Copyright, Designer and Patents Act 1988.

All rights reserved. No part of this publication may be reproduced, stored in a retrieval system or transmitted in any form or by any means, electronic or mechanical, including photocopying, recording or any information storage or retrieval system without the prior permission of the copyright owner.

Printed by Imprint Digital, Exeter, Devon

Book and cover design by Andy Dark

ISBN: 978-1-9191650-0-4

Papillote Press
23 Rozel Road,
London SW4 0EY,
United Kingdom
And Trafalgar, Dominica
www.papillotepress.co.uk

"I came to literature and the literary life through an early love of reading which has never waned. Derek Walcott's verse has been a primary source of sustenance and I admire the magnanimity of Dunstan St Omer's murals immensely."

IRVIN DESIR

Some of these poems have been published in the
following collections:

Confluence: nine St. Lucian poets Edited by Kendel Hippolyte.
Castries: The Source, 1988, pp32-37.

*Roseau Valley and other poems for Brother George Odlum:
an Anthology* Compiled and edited by John Robert Lee.
Castries: Jubilee Trust Fund, 2003, pp19, 20.

Sent Lisi: Poems and Art of Saint Lucia Selected by Kendel
Hippolyte, Jane King, John Robert Lee, Vladimir Lucien.
Castries: Cultural Development Foundation, 2014, pp116, 117.

Acknowledgements

Huge and grateful thanks to Polly Pattullo and Papillote Press for bringing
this talented writer's work to light at last.
The cover is based on an original design by the late Maria Grech.

CONTENTS

INTRODUCTION by Vladimir Lucien 1

ISLANDER
i. The sea wind stirred and roamed upon the water.... 8
ii. The dreaming manchild staring 9
iii. Weaned and honed on sun and song 10
iv. you emerged at the end of dawn dressed in orange 11
v. Through the long day 12
vi. Then one afternoon, after the clink of mugs 13
vii. I shall see you through the cold shoreline 14
viii. She thinks: 15
ix. As a gray, gray villager worn by this world her head 16
x. No friend there 17
xi. Memory returns, like the wind 18
xii. Dark, and branches huddled in darkness 19
xiii. All the good that fares from You 20
xiv. the harried heart 21
xv. But the sun shall settle down on all this 22
xvi. Where I heard nothing hearing only the wind 23

ETUDES
i. So as to leave no chink, no aperture for them to 26
ii. His first memory was music and the practice of painting 27
iii. And so You have recalled Your cup 28

UNPUBLISHED POEMS
The Call 32
A Game of Solitaire 33
Avenues 34
Requiem 35

NOTES ON IRVIN DESIR
John Robert Lee, Kendel Hippolyte, Laurena Primus 40

Introduction:
The Great Silence

by Vladimir Lucien

"For the great silence closes in like a flower..."
                                                    IRVIN DESIR

Upon discovering the work of Irvin Desir, one of my first thoughts must have been: Saint Lucia is too small to have a forgotten or unknown poet who is just being "discovered". For me it was exciting – it made my island seem like the larger literary landscapes that had the benefit of being well documented. It was when I read John Robert Lee's *Bibliography of Saint Lucian Literature* that I realised: people are always writing. Or certainly, Saint Lucians always are – always shining their little personal lights of perception toward life. But Irvin Desir's verse was different, was something else entirely. Less of a light than a silence by turns populating itself and unpopulating itself, and just barely peopling itself with something distinguishable as "man". He says:

The green forest is, where
one may walk through all eternity in a single day (8)

In Desir's work, there is often the noise of life building itself, non-human life, which is so often more of a visual noise working in silence. This is a strange kind of metaphor for he himself, one who was known to be deeply introverted and not often seen in the circles one expects to see a writer of such prodigious talent. In fact, after some time, not seen often at all. In the poetry, it is always in the midst of life's autogenesis that we find, with a soft, vulnerable and fickle presence – man:

> *blood petals roar in the wind*
> *a blue haze hangs on the hill*
> *dawn shimmers with liturgical bells and*
> *the brightness builds, the drifting sky*
> *brushed with blue is deep as history.*
>
> *He would return to the room, read, record*
> *until a clinging weariness whirred the*
> *leaves of his eyes (9)*

Man – that solitary man – is always on the verge of being permanently imbricated by the world around him, especially in the long poem "Islander" that begins the book (and which, for me, is its centre). But it is this that gives us a deeper sense of this "man", because he seems completely unafraid of this prospect of his own dispensability. He is, evidently, a spiritual man – but more in the sense of speaking his actual, inevitable existence than a chosen faith. He is a spirit-man/manspirit. When he speaks, he seems to be speaking not just to someone else, but someone *other*, some spontaneous appearance in his lonely world whom his talking to could easily seem like him – manspirit – talking to himself, his interlocutor as susceptible to disappearance as he is:

> *You should dance, and so you should dance*
> *you turn and rinse long hands of rain;*
> *around the coast all your companions are rooted (11)*

When people appear, they are seen in a vague haze of suspicion:

Then one afternoon, after the clink of mugs
after the doors and dresses that revolve

after the heady group of actors seesawing down
the roads and masks and myriad merging hands. (13)

The poetry is thick with metaphor of nature and vague hints of "civilisation". Its voice emerges from a place that is frighteningly quiet, steady in its observation, casting "a cold eye", as WB Yeats would say, on life. Its placement in time and place is entirely unclear – it does not feel like a time that calendars can account for. It does not feel like a place maps can situate. And this is not because it is not situated in a time that calendars do or did account for, or places that maps contain. This feeling of a certain timelessness and placelessness has something to do with where the poet situates us, his readers. Perhaps by virtue of that thickness of metaphor and that quiet sparseness of human presence, we find ourselves situated in one of two places. We are either situated somewhere in that quiet, hidden place from which the persona looks out at the world, sitting beside us, but not talking to us, or – perhaps even more disconcerting – we are walking around in the poetry itself, having no clue about where to go or turn, being observed by the persona for whom we are but vague, inconsequential presences. If I am to make reference to a local influence, it is definitely Derek Walcott but Walcott's world, for all its metaphor of the natural world, is a "social world"; nature draws its metaphors from the world of man via the poet, the poet is *humanly* present in his observation of nature. The poet wants to interact with what he sees as the "social world" around him. Nature is beautiful and more than tolerant of man. In Desir's world, the man who is not manspirit, is promptly taken over by nature:

wherever we search, death haunts us...

our words fade, fade like mist over mountain
our words add to the silence like lifting dust (14)

It is we who draw the metaphors of our lives from nature. In "Etudes", the second section, the voice that already was lonely as a prophet in his own land, rises. The manspirit is talking to his chief Interlocutor directly, reflecting on what it sees around it: again the transient presence of the man who does not know he is also spirit:

ah night city, city of littered doors
the derelicts curled on cardboard boxes
barren beneath the harvest moon
oblivious even of its own oblivion
the stone flesh dreams on soft stone. (28)

The brief section, "Etudes", closes on that note: "stone flesh dream[ing] on soft stone".

The book closes with a series of unpublished poems. The tone of the first and second sections however abides throughout. Our persona is self-effacing, for the one face he focuses on is one that cannot truly be seen – the face of God. The sense too of the writer's own sparse biography haunts the work, for it seems that he, in observing with such precision that which lay before him, became increasingly aware of his transience:

May it not annoy you in its aim,
Or darken the face that it defends
Nor deem its going an idle game

Nor root for words it will not find
Nor turn HIS nostrils as it ascends
this leave taking lament of mine. (35)

There is also, as the title of the second "Etudes" suggests, a sense throughout of the poet as one who is apprenticing himself, as one who is mastering technically, the metaphor, just as he is, in life, apprenticing himself to spirit, to God and his manifestation in the natural world.

There is something poignant, real and bracing about such a publication. Its humanity is in the very unfinishedness of such a posthumous putting together of work of one who had virtually disappeared.

Its humanity is in that exulting in metaphor, in the wonders it can lead us to, the sense of experimenting with words, with life. And like all lives, there are flourishes of what we spend forever surging towards. The Divine? Sublime? Whatever it is shows up in this brief work quite often. We cannot but worship at the altar of a line such as:

"You filled this cluttered room like
a handful of clove. (16)

And the man behind that line? Gone into the greater mystery of which his own life was a microcosm.

Islander

i

The sea wind stirred and roamed upon the water...
I passed from the spendthrift counting his commandments
the hypocritical, stuttering unbeliever
confession of a woman quilted with untruths.
The green forest is, where
one may walk through all eternity in a single day,
blest with tearing vines and flurried beasts.

So that the cracked bell and the singing may begin
the song goes flaming even as these orange meteors
around this airless, waterless, this sordid drum of earth.
The marauding prodigal returns, the impetuous sea stays
with a motion, rotted seeds of the garden resurge,
weary tendrils fare wildly over fences,
the raucous dun houses stand like sentinels in a row.

ii

The dreaming manchild staring above the
sill leaned into the open:

blood petals roar in the wind
a blue haze hangs on the hill
dawn shimmers with liturgical bells and
the brightness builds, the drifting sky
brushed with blue is deep as history.

He would return to the room, read, record,
until a clinging weariness whirred the
leaves of his eyes;
no calendars kept the years, the years
reverbed, direct beads of an abacus.

Old man, let the crucifixion and the child alone
that the morning moon or his proclamation come.

iii

Weaned and honed on sun and song
they yearn always for greenness
who strewed the rust-coloured leaf of summer
and ran in its wake,
who wearied the shore's straggling by rote,
silver sickled moon on that shore.

Driven the fireflies heave for heaven
the wood doves wait intransit to heaven.
It will come, they shall return.
Heaven is the marsh they have mistaken for home.

iv

you emerged at the end of dawn dressed in orange
self-effacing as a sea wrapped in blue
repeating the high heavens.
You should dance and so you should dance
you turn and rinse long hands of rain;
around the coast all your companions are rooted,
the rain drums, the coffee sheds its bitter beads,
the beachhead heaves its sigh of spume,
whosoever rails at the sea "whore, whore" shall not rest
in the green plantations.

V

Through the long day
you wait within:
crowded alleyways and bars

the echoing vehicular air
possessed and dispossessed
oblivious of your passing.

To reflect on this as return
to primordial time, as a bell
would toll and toll, its strain

is all that happens;
it fires the brightness
with its freedom.

Garnered words
like leaves
glisten on the tree of man.

vi

Then one afternoon, after the clink of mugs
after the doors and dresses that revolve

after the heady group of actors seesawing down
the road and masks and myriad merging of hands,

he could bill you with his hand and rock you,
melt the steel, outstare the blue horizon.

vii

I shall see you through the cold shoreline
where the wind carries and slides over the sand

wherever we search death haunts us
everywhere the distracted petals have gone

our words fade, fade like mist over the mountain
our words add to the silence like lifting dust.

viii

She thinks:

"once a whirled bead at the beck of their skilled fingers
i no longer go into rooms, riven, grieved.
i am no longer startled at the daylight.
The evening lingers in the shade of trees swung by their branches
i wouldn't harm the evening with humming doleful songs:
the spinning dust touches down as so many dreams,
the shredded days shall be (after the separate darknesses)
one interminable day,
and i shall bask in him, inhabit him like this riffled sonorous
shade of the varied blowing bougainvillea i rarely move from,
for it rustles whatever is, whatever reels within.
A withdrawn wanderer on an almond-leaf-littered beach
is as much of it as my mind may imagine him,
and so the freshly fallen grapes of an October evening
bless the fringes of an island I would not abandon.

For the great silence closes in like a flower
and you may once more see, the tree and the light
as it grows, the wavering afternoon as it turns to dusk,
and bread and wine may take us through eternity, as you would see."

ix

As a gray, gray villager worn by this world, her head
is swathed with scarves, her waist bound with bandanas, her pail

balances on her head, or carrying this as she comes
rarely spills her sorrow, you are an ocean murmuring

as it moves, you filled this cluttered room like
a handful of clove.

You say scores of friends have swept past like fishscales
modern mechanisms have slurred the pass of wood doves.

Recall the live scene, the chorus, the shrill chanson, far
from being solemn.

X

No friend
there, no unmeaning
word or gesture and then
the leaf's lure only is intelligible.

Sundered, through speakers
speaking, flustered where I can
no longer think, of nothing, of afternoon
as it would open on far cedars breathing in the wind.

It will neither be
because of you or because
of the rain that has come, for the
handful of dust on him, that he became.

What would come comes
without our knowing, at daylight,
at dusk, revelation shaken from the
undergrowth, still petals spinning at its seam.

xi

Memory returns, like the wind
its leaves of earlier instances
returns like the heaving rain on
arid plains and arid settlements.

Not only you alone, it is the green
day and the ripe dusk that had gone
beating through the air like birds,
the serpent grew thistles where I was growing.

Through shuttered windows
which wind has thrown open, look!
it is not the brightness that goes
it is the blue hill that grows deep.

xii

Dark, and branches huddled in darkness
wave ripe secrets over the soil
the wiry farer rives a way for his stumbling foal,

the one will weary, go breathless,
grow old before another speaks "islander" and learns
"enduring", who limps along where even words

are not vouchsafed, only moonbeam and bell-
murmuring of proud prodigals
worn by wind blast and left on desert trails.

Already the day is reddening,
wind rhetoric between rattled twigs
wind rhetoric between rattling twigs –

failure's Marseillaise.
Then the fettering dew will
fade into the leaf and moon shadow mend the hill.

xiii

All the good that fares from You
who catalyse with fervid hands:
the long drawn out afternoon
womb we may return to
the swift railing of the water
the oasis that would encase the soul.

O fiery fruit! O sufficient rose sunset!
and arms of oak and eyes serene with suffering
the day is Yours, the hour that fades and fading
grows into evening, the room is Yours; and even as
these primordial suns rolling into enclaves of the
sea that continues – he hums he reads You.

xiv

the harried heart
spurns the superfluous
mob obscuring the mountain

carious characters of friends
the warped insufferable aged
twin scales of a single truth

weighed our coming
close, our remonstrance, chipped
from twin slabs of stone

heart hurrying our deaths
our stream of word over stone,
nothing gnaws the air

nothing swirls out of sight
like a bruised seabird
crack of water in the rock

wind and wave turn
indifferently,
it drizzles, you inch away.

XV

But the sun shall settle down on all this

indelibly and there as the early day

where sun and the silence reigned

where the tree bared its arms

where long love and the mountain moved

where the ocean nurtured and churned in its bed

slow skeletal seed of my grandfathers

that the blest moon may be summoned down

the heaven of clouds and stars may be heard

hearkening suns might detach from the sea

beseeching winds be seen at a distance

xvi

Where I heard nothing hearing only the wind
sea wind flailing the elate lettered leaves
like serial toys or memoirs or years

nothing now quite reaches this no reminiscence
memory studded with the qualms of years flows
soundless and far distant as an ocean within

there's no forgetting blind almonds strewn on sand
gargling seagulls and pebbles from lips of the sea
the gold breath of the water the glimmering evening air

you level your head you shake the sand from your shoes
free the separated self of trivia and semblances
move on – seal the lip, lock the lid and their remembrances.

Etudes

To the first muralist, Apilo
(Dunstan St. Omer 1927 - 2015)

i

so as to leave no chink, no aperture for them to
slip in again, it is robed in darkness, death,
it whimpers at absurdities, slices truth to taste
and trips along; by now its barnacled feet strike sand-
stone, it doubles on its knees and winces, stares over its
shoulder and winces, trembling, weighing its lids like balm.

the animal drools and makes its way
amid tidemarks of daylight lingering on sand
tree trunks there like disgruntled men
sea wind struggling across sea
and settles down on shifting sand tired of
thinking, but now a new thought attracts it
as looking along the level sea
it sees or thinks it sees
like wobbling waves in the near
distance: dolphins, happy in the daylight.

ii

his first memory was music and the practice of painting
now memories were muddled, the dream shorn.

why now must bird through eye of storm?
why blind cataracts find and confound him?

why swimming stones wind up on shore?
retreating waves return to haunt them there?

i must remember Vincent & the dilating fields of dawn
i must remember Hobbema & the narrowing road at Middelharnis
i must remember Piranesi & the eerie elephantine prison
i must remember Goya & the splayed hands of heroes

> o dead! pray for those who
> stagger when they walk,
> those who whisper intimacies
> into the night that will not end
>
> and rain that will not fall
> like a shower of sand
> reducing to nothing the
> nameless fears

o violins ignoring ignorance! o determinable waters!
the river ran on and drowned all signs of death.

iii

and so You have recalled Your cup, withdrawn
Your wrath – those bridges he had burnt –
and turned the swineherd seaward.

son of man, the revolving wheels of days
the tongues turning on themselves
the hater-jester standing grinning over the dark river
recede from memory like tresses of the waves.
the flute-charmed python curled its spleen. Selah.

and so the song pushes through the plague
becomes held leaves, houses on the hill
becomes loud litanies, pinches of sage-brush, things.

ah night city, city of littered doors
the derelicts curled on cardboard boxes
barren beneath the harvest moon
oblivious even of its own oblivion
the stone flesh dreams on soft stone

Opposite page: Irvin Desir's original handwritten version.
The printed version (above) is slightly different.

III

and so You have recalled Your cup, withdrawn
Your wrath —those bridges he had burnt—
and turned the swineherd seaward

Son of Man, the revolving wheels of days
the tongues turning on themselves
the hater-jester standing grinning over the dark river
recede from memory like tresses of the waves.
the flute charmed python curled its spleen   selah

and so the song pushes through the plague
becomes held leaves, houses on the hill
becomes loud litanies, pinches of sage-brush, things.

ah night city, city of littered doors
the derelicts curled on cardboard boxes,
empty beneath the harvest moon
oblivious even of its own oblivion
the stone flesh dreams on soft stone

IRVIN DÉSIR

Unpublished poems

The Call

(for Patricia Charles, 1936-2010)

Hold your heart off your sleeve,
See, and scribble to believe,
Go through your treasure trove,
Give, and give to the GOD above

Tried, reiterated prayer overwhelms like logarithms,
So much so we forget our first intent:
Our wants we are wont to invent.
Cut off from things, dim times, flourishing customs

Longings loom large,
Heave from raw shoreline to horizon;
But there is no skiff, shallop or barge
To which our trawled, desisting steps are driven.

Hold your heart off your sleeve,
See, and scribble to believe,
Go, through your treasure trove,
Give, and give to the GOD above.

A Game of Solitaire

Wary of a rebuff,
He plays deaf-mute and anonymous,
As if not cut from the same cloth
Although a fixture and pasted to the place.

And even more removed than the rest,
Ever on the fringes,
Considers the card players
Slamming what is better, best.

Avenues

I don't remember how many
They were: they mass and mass and it's an old city
Avenues on avenues where memories grow old
The bowed and wrinkled sweep the coal
Of bonfires. And grey solid stone buildings
That cling.
And an old man beneath a wooden bench froze
With sleep.
I grope for a certain refrain: in vacant wind-swept
Avenues, days and nights and days.

Requiem

1

May it not annoy you in its aim,
Or darken the face that it defends,
Nor deem its going an idle game

Nor root for words it will not find,
Nor turn HIS nostrils as it ascends,
This leave taking lament of mine.

ii

The face over mine; the riven mask;
The voice warning me to wake;
Work that is a thankless task,
There is so much at stake.

Long before you breathed your last
What did you *not* relinquish?
Or what did you not distinguish
Keeping close a thought for others as you passed?

iii

With all this starting from within,
What the finishing worm shall not prey upon;
One searching for her sons
And sharing all that she remains

2

Here's one bent on hammering
Stars' silver into quick cash,
Imagine being bent on painting
Amid such murderous trash.

Another, instead of the trade,
Clock work or work in silver, in gold,
Walks bowed and bewildered
Carrying two two-dollar tins of coal.

ii

When I am dead, you will know!
Just as you said, just so

And come to know as well,
His every word and move, a virtual call,
A cue, a prelude to hell.

3

At first they were closed, puzzling, or plain dumb,
The cruelly composed faces in Bosch's *Temptation*
Those suddenly at your bedside were the same,
Near kin, bent nun or lilliputian,
And, ever the maverick, one among them,
Sharper, smoother, more politic than the rest,

From the door of an adjoining room
Cranes his neck and scans on your face.

        4

There and not there,
Hemmed in by scum,
You wrestle with prayer,
One invalid in one room

ii

Their throwing words at you,
Searching to irk your spirit.
Old climber low and low.
The suave savant just plain spit.

iii

When do they slip into their own,
Squirrels of other lives and yours,
Once yoked to you and you alone,
Lifting felicities like leftovers?

iv
This crippling perplexity,
Hesitation before hounds,
Telling beads into infinity,
Folding, unfolding your hands

v

You strain your substance
Listening to what you were;
What follows is abundance
Of shades and shadows as they are.

                5
But, Gie George, Miss Marge, Milly St. Rose,
Naming you now I can close;

From the first
Chorus to the very last,
Still standing when the curtain folds,
You real, working, herculean souls

Gie George, Miss Marge, Milly St. Rose,
Naming you now I can close.

Notes on Irvin Desir

Irvin Desir was born on 13 December 1954 in Castries, Saint Lucia, to Mary Una and Joseph Haze Desir. He was the fourth of five children – three boys and two girls. He was educated at St Aloysius RC Boys' School and St Mary's College in St Lucia. He spent time with his sister Merle in Barbados and also lived in Martinique. He died in Castries on 4 September 2024.

John Robert Lee writes:
I spent much time with Irvin Desir in the 1970s and 1980s, more than 40 years ago. So memory blurs as I try to recall our conversations and the times enjoyed together. He would often accompany me and my two daughters to the beach. One evening (a clear memory), a number of us, including the late Gandolph St Clair, were in Irvin's room at his family home at the end of Chaussée Road, Castries, raving over the latest book by Derek Walcott. Could it have been *The Star-Apple Kingdom*? As he wrote at the beginning of this slim volume, Derek and the painter Dunstan St Omer were his local heroes.

Irvin's work was much admired by Walcott and local poets who were aware of his poems. As witnessed in this collection, the imagery of his lines and their movement were fresh and startling. Some samples: "...the fireflies heave for heaven"; "you turn and rinse long hands of rain."; a personal favourite is this one: "you filled this cluttered room like/a handful of clove." And, "the leaf's lure only is intelligible."

He was very well read and the French classics were among his favourites. His poems reflect his readings of St John Perse, Aimé Césaire, French symbolists as well as Walcott, TS Eliot, WB Yeats. As he wrote, he came to literature and the literary life through an early love of reading which never waned.

Kendel Hippolyte and I unsuccessfully tried to get a chapbook published for Irvin from 1986. We had a cover designed by the late Maria Grech, which we have kept in a slightly modified form for this edition. I am not sure why publication never happened, even as we were able to publish several works of our own and a number of anthologies of Saint Lucian poems in which Irvin's work was included.

Inevitably, family and work responsibilities, travel, Irvin's own health and other situations meant that we lost touch. We would meet only occasionally. His places of residence seemed to change. Queries about his writing were met with vague responses. Not many of our earlier acquaintances seemed to know where he lived or what was happening to him. And then, sometime in September 2024, I see an obituary notice announcing his passing.

Irvin deserves his placing among Saint Lucian, Caribbean and other poets, no matter how modest his literary legacy and the unfulfilled promise of his genuine poetic gift.

Kendel Hippolyte writes:

Irving Desir was always … singular, intent. I don't mean grim or scowling – nothing like that. But when I turn to memories of him walking Castries streets, the image is of someone focused. Not at all oblivious to the normal busyness around him, but going through it to some destination not quite connected with it. And I'm checking my memory and imagination now to see if I'm just romanticising – but I'm not. Trying to remember if I ever saw him ambling. No.

We didn't spend a lot of time in each other's company, just that the time was always good time and occasionally with a feeling of out of time. Because there weren't – and aren't – many people you can casually sit with on the floor of an upstairs side veranda above a busy intersection of one the busiest communities in Castries, Marchand, and chat freestyle about Césaire as though it's the natural thing to do on a Saturday morning. Strangely, we seldom discussed his own poetry. There was a mutual regard for each other's work, occasionally voiced in a casual comment, but no up front workshop style conversations about it. Once we did a reading of a fragment of a play he was working on. A lot of fun because the scene was a group of men playing dominoes and the dialogue zigzagged between whatever they were discussing and the exclamations and humorous taunts of a Saint Lucian domino game. Did he ever finish the play? My feeling is he didn't, though of course I wish otherwise; it showed his keen observation of and relish in the urban folkways of the community he lived in. His poetry had a different texture, came from a different plane.

Derek Walcott had a high regard for his work and one of the heaviest moments I remember is during a brief conversation when he asked me how Irvin's work was going and I gave a cautious answer and he replied, "You may be looking at someone who's stopped writing." The statement lodged deep. It became the title of a very brief poem I wrote for Irvin.

Remembering him, though, the most luminous memory is of an occasion when he was at our home in Pavée and he was intoning his poems to Jane King and I and someone else who was most likely John Robert Lee. "Intoning" is the only word that can convey the aurality, the aura, of the experience. He had the slim manuscript in his hands but seldom looked at it. Seldom looked at us. Looked at the wall behind us, over our heads – that's how I remember it. "Beyond us" is probably the most accurate way to express it. Perhaps the most accurate image of him too.

Laurena Primus, a niece of Irvin Desir and the executor of his estate, remembers her uncle:
As a teenager, I recalled Uncle Irvin visiting us often, especially since we lived near our grandfather's home. I was about 16 then. He encouraged me to read poetry and often shared reflections on his own writing – always thoughtful, and quietly intense. Although he was working – at times for Radio St Lucia – while I was still in school, he would occasionally take time to help with my homework and speak to me about literature, gently guiding me toward a deeper appreciation for language.

His brother Keith fondly remembers Irvin as a voracious reader and a deeply committed writer – one who remained faithful to his creative voice despite life's many challenges. As Keith once put it, "Irvin's poetry was difficult and deep – and it didn't rhyme."

In the spirit of honouring that voice, this collection of Irvin's poetry is being published posthumously through the loving efforts of some of his dearest friends, including John Robert Lee and Kendel Hippolyte. They knew his heart, his struggles, and the depth of his craft. With care and quiet determination, they worked to ensure that Irvin's words would not be forgotten. Thanks to their commitment – and with the support of Papillote Press – his poetry now finds its way into the world, just as he would have wanted. Their collaboration ensures that Irvin's singular voice and vision will live on, offering readers the chance to engage with the profound, unconventional, and unflinching truths that shaped his work.

He is survived by his sister, Angelique Desir, his brother, Keith Desir, and a host of nieces and nephews who cherish his presence and spirit.